DISCOVER  SCIENCE
LIGHT

Kim Taylor

Chrysalis Children's Books

DISCOVER ● SCIENCE

Contents

This edition published in 2003 by
 Chrysalis Children's Books
64 Brewery Road, London N7 9NT

Copyright © Chrysalis Books PLC
Text © Kim Taylor Times Four Publishing Ltd
Photographs © Kim Taylor and Jane Burton
(except where credited elsewhere)

A Belitha Book

ISBN 1 84138 618 9

Designed by Robin Wright, Times Four Publishing Ltd

Illustrated by Guy Smith

Science adviser: Richard Oels, Warden Park School,
Cuckfield, Sussex

Origination by Bright Arts, Hong Kong

Typeset by Amber Graphics, Burgess Hill

Printed in Hong Kong

About this book

On every page of this book you will find fascinating photographs to help you understand what light is and how it works.

You will also find the answer to many intriguing questions. For example, do you know why the sky is blue – or why it is not blue but black when you view it from the Moon? Have you ever wondered why rainbows happen? Do you know why things look red – or green, or blue, or any other colour?

Alongside each topic you will find a simple experiment to help you have fun while discovering more about light. For example, you can make your own rainbow, record the movement of the Sun, find out where the blind spot is in your eye, or carry out some surprising colour experiments by moonlight!

Sunlight

All our daylight comes from the Sun. It takes about eight minutes for the Sun's rays to reach the Earth. The Sun's rays are made up of very very fast **electro-magnetic** vibrations. The number of vibrations per second controls the colour of the light. Of the colours you can see, violet has the most vibrations per second and red has the least. You cannot see rays with fewer vibrations per second than red light, but you can feel them as heat.

White light

Light from the Sun contains all the colours. When the colours are mixed together, they make white light. Here you can see the colours in sunlight. They have been separated by a filter on the camera lens.

Taking in light

Something that is black soaks up, or absorbs, all colours of light. Something that is red, like this pepper, absorbs all colours except red, which is reflected.

Reflecting light

Something that is white reflects all colours of light. The light bounces off it in all directions. This lemon absorbs other colours but reflects yellow light.

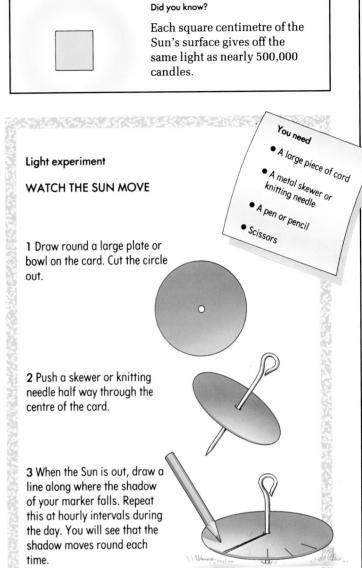
A light bulb changes electricity into heat and light. Inside the bulb is a thin wire. Electricity flows through the wire and makes it very hot until it glows. Electric light contains more red and yellow than sunlight.

Light experiment

WATCH THE SUN MOVE

You need
- A large piece of card
- A metal skewer or knitting needle
- A pen or pencil
- Scissors

1 Draw round a large plate or bowl on the card. Cut the circle out.

2 Push a skewer or knitting needle half way through the centre of the card.

3 When the Sun is out, draw a line along where the shadow of your marker falls. Repeat this at hourly intervals during the day. You will see that the shadow moves round each time.

Pigments

Pigments are chemicals that absorb the light of some colours and reflect other colours. This avocado pear has green pigment in its skin. It reflects only green light.

Paints

Paints contain pigments made from plants, ground up rocks or chemicals. This ball is painted with a pigment that reflects only blue light.

Eyes and light

Your eyes work like a camera. When you look at something, light enters your eyes through a hole in each eyeball. It passes through a **lens** (see page 20) and is focused on the back of the eyeball. Messages about the light then pass to your brain. Your brain works out what you are looking at and how far away it is.

Human eyes are good at seeing, but some animals, such as birds of prey, can see better. Some creatures have poor vision. The woodlouse, for example, can see only light and dark. Moles can hardly see anything at all. They do not need to see well because they spend almost all their time in darkness under the ground.

Insect eyes

Insect eyes, like this horsefly's, are made up of many tiny eyes clustered together like a honeycomb. Each lens sees a different part of the scene, so the insect can see in many directions at once.

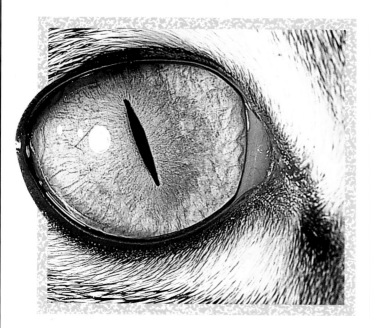

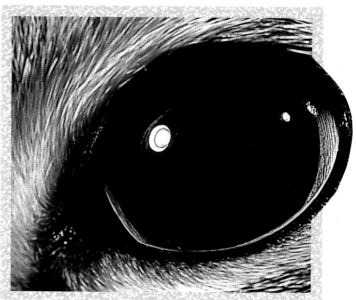

How eyes work

The coloured part of your eye is called the **iris**. In the centre of the iris is a black hole called the **pupil**. The iris controls the amount of light coming in by altering the size of the pupil.

The pictures of a cat's eyes above show how eyes work. On the left, the pupil closes to a thin slit when the light is bright. On the right you can see how large the pupil gets when the light is dim.

6

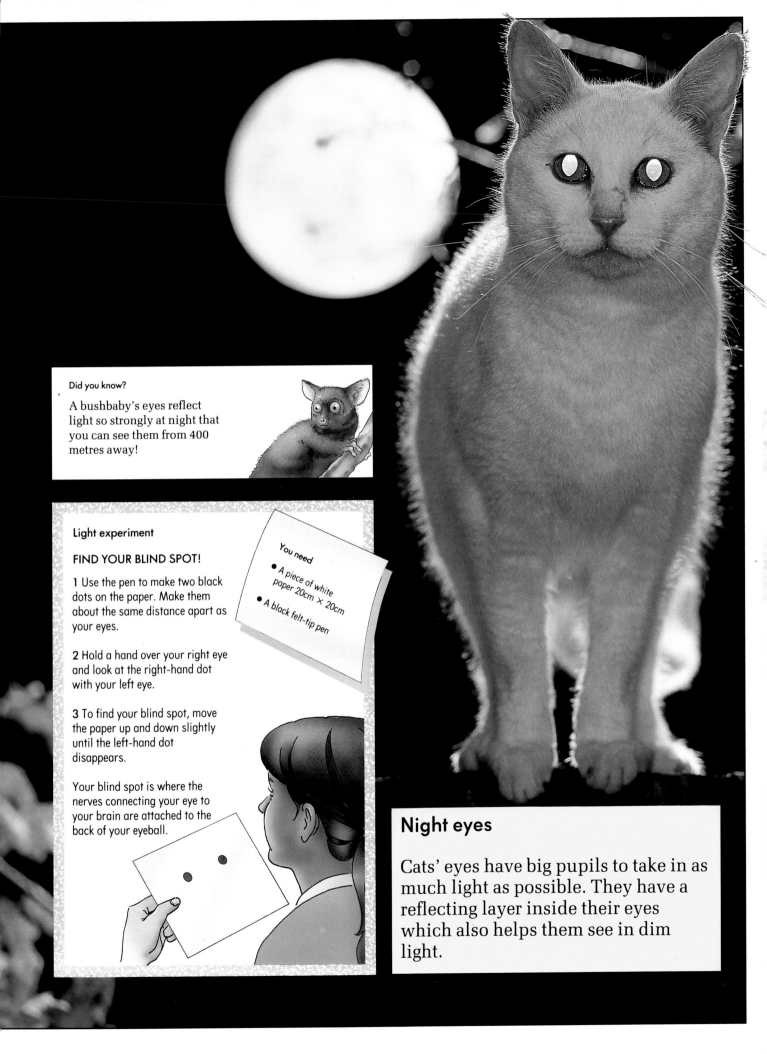

Light experiment

FIND YOUR BLIND SPOT!

1 Use the pen to make two black dots on the paper. Make them about the same distance apart as your eyes.

2 Hold a hand over your right eye and look at the right-hand dot with your left eye.

3 To find your blind spot, move the paper up and down slightly until the left-hand dot disappears.

Your blind spot is where the nerves connecting your eye to your brain are attached to the back of your eyeball.

You need

- A piece of white paper 20cm × 20cm
- A black felt-tip pen

Night eyes

Cats' eyes have big pupils to take in as much light as possible. They have a reflecting layer inside their eyes which also helps them see in dim light.

Skylight

Rays of light are rather like millions of tiny bouncy balls. If you throw the balls down on to uneven stony ground, they will bounce in all directions. They are **scattered**. Sunlight is scattered like this when it hits a cloud. The light bounces off in all directions from the water droplets in the cloud. Some of the light bounces back into space and some is never as bright on a cloudy day as it is when the Sun is shining.

If you hold a piece of white paper between you and an electric light, you will see how the light is scattered in a similar way.

Sunrise and sunset

The colours you sometimes see at sunrise or sunset are caused by dust, smoke or water droplets which scatter light in a different way.

Blue skies

Light is scattered by almost anything it hits, even air. Air scatters blue light but not other colours in the Sun's rays. This is why the sky looks blue. On the Moon, which has no air, the scorching Sun shines out of an inky black sky because the Sun's light shines straight through without being scattered. Close to the Earth, dust and water particles in the air scatter other colours than blue, making the sky paler near to the horizon.

Did you know?

At the top of Mount Everest the air is so thin that light passes through without being scattered. This makes the sky look black!

Light experiment

LIGHT BLOCK!

You need
- Two pairs of polarizing sunglasses

1 Hold the glasses level, with the left lens of one pair in front of the right lens of the other.

2 Slowly rotate one pair of glasses about 90° until light is gradually blocked out.

Polarizing glasses normally block light that is vibrating up and down, but let through light that vibrates from side to side. When the lenses are at right-angles to each other, they block both kinds of light.

Only blue light is scattered high in the sky. Lower down, other colours are scattered. That is why the sky looks paler near the horizon.

In the red

When the Sun is close to the horizon, it has to shine through more than 100km of air. Even a little smoke in the air changes the Sun's colour.

Blue and green cannot get through the smoky air and are blocked, but red light can still get through. This is why the Sun often looks red close to the horizon.

Night light

It is never completely dark, even outside at night. The stars provide enough light for many night animals to hunt by. Owls, foxes and badgers can see in what humans would call darkness. Their eyes and the eyes of many animals are far better than human eyes at seeing in dim light. On cloudy nights the lights from distant towns or cities may be reflected from the undersides of clouds, making it easier to see your way than on clear nights.

Some animals and plants can actually make their own light in the darkness. Their light is made by chemicals. Unlike the light from an electric lamp, the light made by plants and animals is quite cold.

Did you know?

Snakes called pit vipers have little pits between their eyes and nostrils to detect infra-red rays given off by their warm-blooded prey.

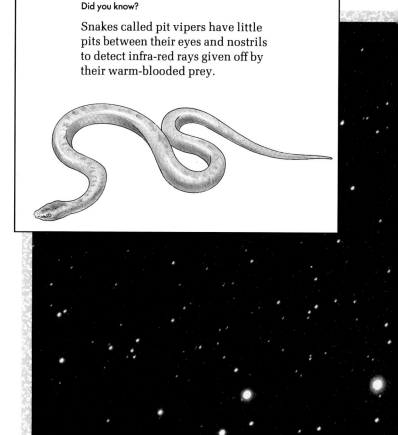

Luminous logs!

In the autumn, brown toadstools called honey fungus grow on some rotten logs. The fungus forms a network of white threads inside the log.

If a log with honey fungus on it is split open, parts of it are **luminous**. At night a green glow is made by oxygen in the air mixing with chemicals in the fungus.

Moonlight

The Moon shines brightly at night but it has no light of its own. Its surface is all stones and dust. This desert is lit by the brilliant Sun, so the moonlight we see is really reflected sunlight. But the Moon does not reflect light like a mirror. To understand how moonlight works, point a lamp with a metal shade away from a wall. Hold a piece of white paper about 30cm in front of the lamp. Light reflected from the paper lights up the wall. When the Moon is a thin crescent you can sometimes see the rest of its shape very faintly. The crescent is made by direct sunlight, while the faint shape is made by sunlight reflected from the Earth back to the Moon.

A photograph of the Moon taken from space.

Glow-worms

Female glow-worms give off a greenish glow at night to attract males. The glow-worm's body contains chemicals that make the glowing light.

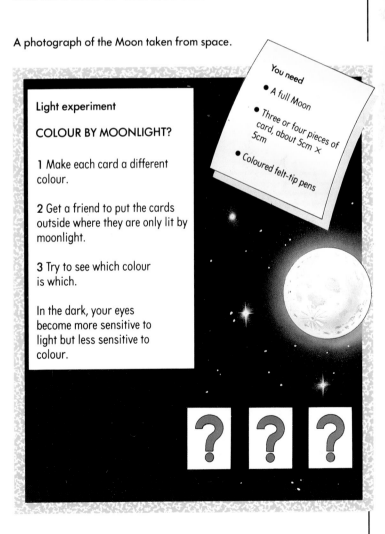

Light experiment

COLOUR BY MOONLIGHT?

1 Make each card a different colour.

2 Get a friend to put the cards outside where they are only lit by moonlight.

3 Try to see which colour is which.

In the dark, your eyes become more sensitive to light but less sensitive to colour.

You need

● A full Moon

● Three or four pieces of card, about 5cm × 5cm

● Coloured felt-tip pens

11

Brightness

Light from a candle, an electric lamp or the Sun **radiates**. This means that the light travels from its source in straight lines in all directions. Light which radiates gets dimmer the further away you are from its source. Suppose you were reading this page using just one candle in a dark room. If you moved twice as far away from the candle, its light would only be a quarter as bright. Move twice as close to the candle and its light is four times as bright! Light from the Sun works in the same way. On Earth, the Sun's light is about four times brighter than it is on Mars. This is because Mars is about twice Earth's distance from the Sun.

Saturn

The Sun's light takes 1 hour and 20 minutes to reach Saturn and is only one hundredth as bright as it is on Earth.

Glowing, glowing gone!

It is the Earth spinning round that makes the Sun seem to move across the sky. Near the horizon, dust and smoke in the atmosphere block some of the Sun's light, making it seem dimmer as it sets.

Light years

Light is the fastest thing known. In space, light travels at nearly 300,000km a second! Even at this great speed, it takes eight minutes for the Sun's light to reach us. Remember this next time you see the Sun rise. When it just peeps over the horizon, you are seeing it where it was eight minutes before. The stars are so far away that their light takes not minutes but *years* to reach us. This is why the distance of stars from Earth is measured in light years. The nearest star is over four light years away. **Galaxies** may be millions of light years away.

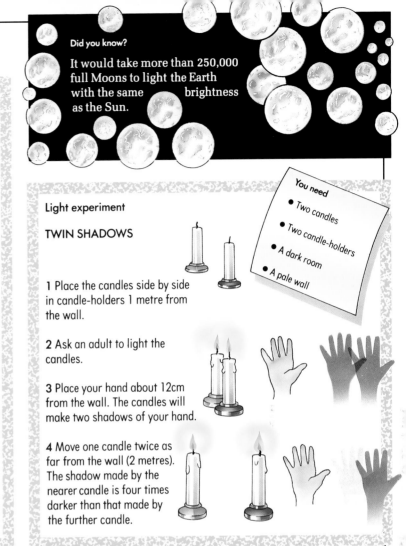

Did you know?

It would take more than 250,000 full Moons to light the Earth with the same brightness as the Sun.

Light experiment

TWIN SHADOWS

You need
- Two candles
- Two candle-holders
- A dark room
- A pale wall

1 Place the candles side by side in candle-holders 1 metre from the wall.

2 Ask an adult to light the candles.

3 Place your hand about 12cm from the wall. The candles will make two shadows of your hand.

4 Move one candle twice as far from the wall (2 metres). The shadow made by the nearer candle is four times darker than that made by the further candle.

Bigger not brighter

This bulb is shining through a hole on to a white board. It makes a rectangle of light on the board. If you move the board further away, the rectangle gets bigger but less bright, because the same amount of light is spread over a wider area.

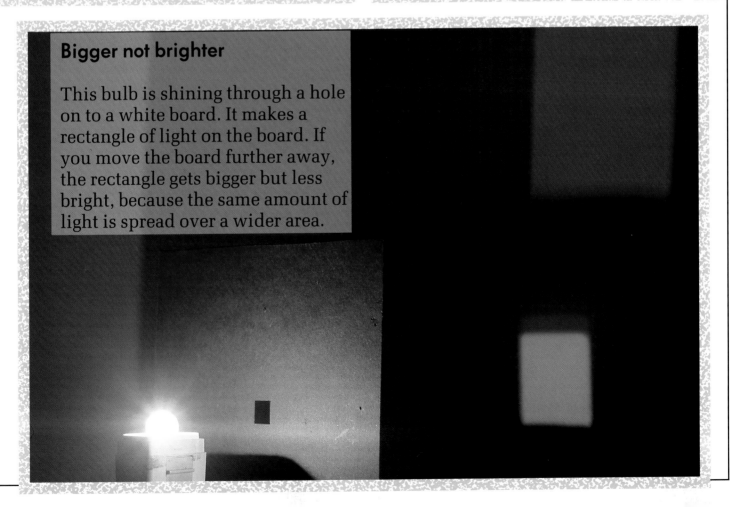

Sunbeams and shadows

When you put your hand in front of an electric lamp you can make a shadow of your hand on a wall. The shadow is not very sharp because the lamp is quite big. A candle flame is smaller and makes a much sharper shadow. The nearer you put your hand to the lamp, the bigger its shadow becomes. This is because light radiates (see page 12). Light from the Sun also radiates but because the Sun is so far away, its rays are almost parallel when they reach the Earth. You would have to move your hand millions of kilometres nearer the Sun before its shadow would start to look bigger!

Smoke drifting across these sunbeams scatters the light so that you can see them.

Sunbeams

If the air was perfectly clear, a beam of light could pass right in front of your eyes and you would not see it. But any tiny particles floating in the air send light scattering in all directions so that some of it enters your eyes. Then you can see the beam. Smoke in the picture on the left makes the sunbeams visible.

When the Sun is low in the sky it makes longer shadows. This kitten's shadow is lit mostly by light from the sky. The blue sky makes the shadow blue.

Did you know?

When the Sun is low in the mountains, you can sometimes see your shadow against the clouds, with a halo of light around it. It looks like a huge monster walking beside you!

Light experiment

LOOK AT A LIGHT BEAM

1 Make a hole in one end of the box. Switch on the torch and place it inside the box so that it shines out through the hole.

2 Gently blow a little talcum powder in front of the hole. The powder will show up brightly wherever it drifts into the beam.

You need
- A torch
- A cardboard box
- Talcum powder
- A dark room

Shadows

When you stand with your back to the Sun you can see your shadow on the ground in front of you. It looks dark but not black. In fact the surrounding sunlit ground is usually up to eight times as bright as your shadow. Your shadow is lit by some reflected light but mostly by skylight.

Haloes, like the one above, are rings of brightness around the Sun or Moon. They are caused by millions of tiny ice crystals in the air which act as **prisms** (see page 18).

15

Reflections

Reflected light is light which is bounced off something. A ray of light reflected from a mirror bounces off in one direction only. It is like throwing a bouncy ball at a smooth floor: the ball always bounces where you expect. However, a ray of light reflected from white paper bounces off in all directions. It is scattered (see page 8). Sometimes you can see the two sorts of reflected light at once. Look at this page and you can see the image of your lamp reflected in its shiny surface. But you can still see the print and pictures shown by scattered light.

Here is a picture of a collie dog named Lark. Notice the shape of the white blaze on her forehead. It is slightly offset to the right – which is her left-hand side.

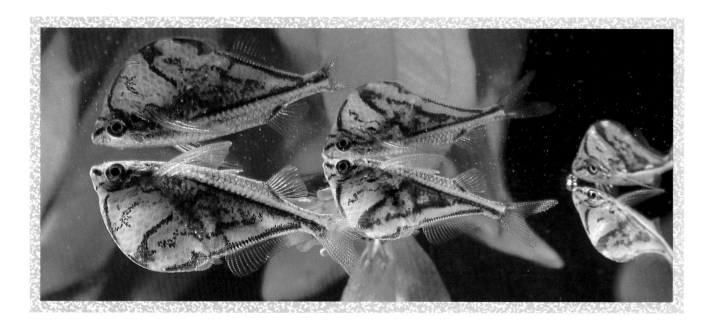

Fish eye view

The underneath of the surface of water reflects better than the top. But it only reflects when you look at it from an angle. If you look straight up at the surface, you see right through it.

A fish looking up at the surface sees a circle of sky. Around the circle is a perfect mirror. These hatchet fish are reflected in the perfect mirror of the under-surface of the water.

This is a mirror-image of Lark. It does not look exactly the same. The blaze is now towards her right. You can see that a mirror-image is the opposite of the real thing.

Did you know?

The angle at which a ray of light strikes a mirror is always the same as the angle at which it is reflected.

Light experiment

SPOT THE DOTS

You need
- Two pocket mirrors
- A die

1 Hold the mirrors facing each other about 15cm apart, with the die between them.

2 Look over the top of one mirror at the other and angle the mirrors until you can see a line of dice.

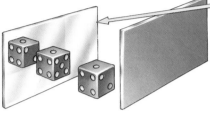

Notice how the reflections show alternate sides of the die.

Water images

The surface of a still pond can act like a mirror. It reflects some, but not all, of the light that falls on it. That is why reflections in water look darker than the real object.

When the pond is covered in ripples, reflections become wobbly. The curves of each ripple reflect the light in different directions. This makes the reflected images stretch and squash into odd shapes.

Prisms

A prism is a triangular block of something clear, such as glass. When a ray of light passes into a prism it is bent at an angle. This bending of light is called **refraction**. When the ray comes out of the other side of the prism it is refracted again. The insides of the prism can act as mirrors. If a ray of light in a prism strikes the side at a fine angle, it does not leave the prism, but is reflected. This is how the under surface of water acts as a mirror (see page 16).

(see page 16)

Light experiment

HOW TO SPLIT LIGHT

You need
- A plastic tub
- A pocket mirror
- Early morning or late afternoon sunshine

1 Fill the tub with water and place it in sunlight coming through a window.

2 Put the mirror in the water and move it at an angle to the Sun until you can see rainbow colours on the wall or the ceiling.

How a prism works

When rays of white light enter and leave the prism they are refracted and split into colours. Some of the rays are reflected by the inside of the prism.

The ray of sunlight from the left is mostly reflected inside the prism so that it bounces back up to the left. The rest of the light is split into rainbow colours.

Splitting light

When sunlight is shone into a prism so that most of it is reflected, the small part of the light that is not reflected is split into rainbow colours. The reason for this is that each colour is refracted at a slightly different angle. Blue is refracted most and red the least. Raindrops refract and reflect light just like thousands of prisms to make a rainbow. (See pages 22-23).

(See pages 22-23).

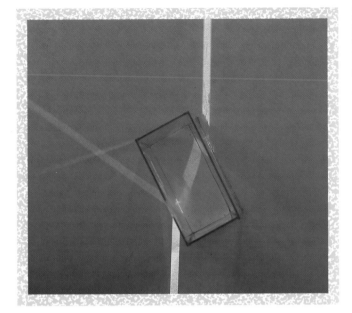

Bending light

Light going into a glass tank of water is bent sideways. When it comes out of the tank it is bent the other way.

Multiple images

A prism with six flat faces placed in front of a camera lens gives a picture of a cat with five fat faces.

The six-legged toad

This toad seems to have six legs, but it is really light playing tricks. Refraction shows you two of the toad's legs twice. Can you see which legs are doubled up? Where you are looking through the water surface at a fine angle, rays of light from the toad's hind legs are refracted downwards so that you see them from the top as well as through the glass from the front.

Water in a glass tank acts as a prism. When you look through the front of the tank and the surface at the same time, the toad seems to have six legs!

Lenses

A lens is like a prism (see page 18), but instead of having flat surfaces its sides are curved. Light is bent when it passes in and out of a lens, just as it is with a prism. Lenses either concentrate light rays so that they **converge**, or spread them out so that they **diverge**. When light rays from one point pass through a lens and converge on to another point, the lens makes an image which is in focus. The distance between the lens and the image it makes of a far-away object is called the **focal length**. Thick lenses with very curved surfaces have short focal lengths. Thin, slightly curved lenses – like spectacle lenses – have long focal lengths.

Natural lenses

Anything clear with a curved surface, such as the raindrop in this picture, can act as a lens. You can see the tiny upside-down image it has made of a flower beyond.

Upside down

The image of this candle flame made by the lens is bigger than the real flame and upside down. The dotted lines show the path of the rays of light which are gathered together by the lens so that they converge. The image of the candle is upside down because the rays of light from the tip and base of the candle are made to cross over by the lens.

Water lenses

Lenses do not have to be round.
Ripples on water have curved surfaces
and can focus sunlight into wavy
patterns on the bottom of a pool.

Did you know?

About 200 years ago,
lacemakers used lenses made
of hollow glass bulbs filled
with water to magnify their
tiny stitches.

Light experiment

MAKE A LENS

1 Fill the jar with water
and screw the lid on
tightly.

2 Roll the jar slowly
over a newspaper and it
will magnify the height of
the print but not the
width.

You need

● An empty jam jar
with a screw-top lid

● Water

● Newspaper

Et haru
tempor
impedit
volupta
autem
atib saepe eveniet ut er

Rainbows

For you to see a rainbow, the Sun must be fairly low in the sky. This is because the rays of light from the Sun to the rainbow and from the rainbow to you are always at an angle of 41°. With a high Sun the rainbow would be in the ground and not in the sky.

A rainbow is part of a circle. You only see the part of the circle that is in the sky – unless you happen to be in an aeroplane. Then it is possible to see the whole rainbow circle.

In a rainbow you can see all the colours of light: red, orange, yellow, green, blue, indigo and violet.

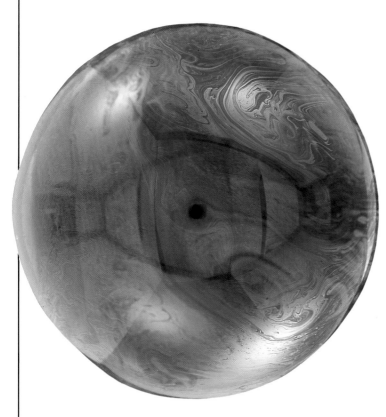

A detergent bubble with rainbow colours caused by its surface skin of water.

How rainbows happen

When raindrops fall through sunlight they act as prisms (see page 18), splitting the light into rainbow colours. The colours shine out of each raindrop in narrow bands. You can only see the colours that are shining directly at you. These come from the drops that are falling through the magic 41°.

Colour film

The rainbow colours in the detergent bubble on the left are not made by prisms. The skin of the bubble is a very thin layer of water which **interferes** with the vibrations of light, making the colours visible.

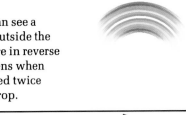

Sometimes you can see a second rainbow outside the first. Its colours are in reverse order. This happens when sunlight is reflected twice inside each raindrop.

Light experiment

MAKE YOUR OWN RAINBOW

You need
- A garden hose attached to a tap
- A sunny day

1 Turn on the hose and adjust it so it gives a very fine spray.

2 Stand with your back to the Sun and direct the spray into the air. This should make a rainbow as the water breaks up the sunlight into different colours.

Rainbow drops

Sunshine makes brilliant colours appear in dew drops which act as prisms.

Rainbow web

The very fine threads of a spider's web act as prisms, splitting the light into colours.

23

Animal colours

Animal colours always have a purpose. Many animals are coloured like their surroundings so that they are difficult to see. This is called **camouflage**. Other animals are very brightly coloured. Bright colours are used as signals. Usually the signals are for other animals of the same sort to see. A blue fish like the one opposite uses its colour to warn other male fish off its territory. The colour of insects such as wasps and ladybirds warns birds that they are not good to eat.

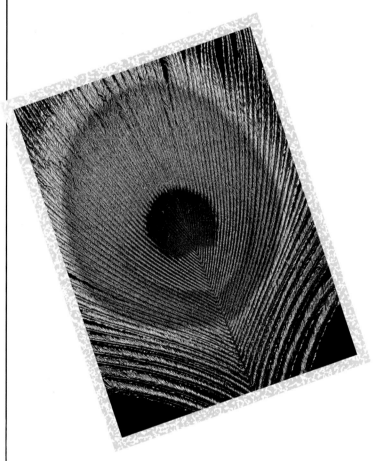

The blue and green in this peacock tail feather are iridescent. The colours you see depend on the angle you hold the feather.

Feathers and scales

Many animals are coloured by pigments (see page 5), but some have colours made in quite a different way. Feathers, fish scales and beetles' backs have minutely thin layers on them which interfere with light vibrations, reflecting some colours and not others. To see these **iridescent** colours in a feather you may have to tilt it at different angles.

Light experiment

FEATHER COLLECTION

Make your own feather collection. You can keep feathers you find by sticking them in a note book with sticky tape. Label them when you have identified which birds they come from. Which birds have iridescent feathers?

You need
- A note book
- Sticky tape
- A pen or pencil

A peacock butterfly. Below is an enlargement of its wing showing the scales which give the wings their colour.

Scaly wings

Butterfly and moth wings are covered with tiny scales that give the wings their colour. Without scales the wings would be clear, like a fly's. The tiny scales are visible in the enlarged picture of a peacock butterfly's wing. Many butterflies, particularly blue and purple ones, have iridescent wing scales. The blue scales of the peacock butterfly are iridescent.

Plant colours

There are very good reasons why plants are coloured. For instance, some berries turn red when they are ripe so that birds can see that they are ready to eat. Plants need birds to eat their berries so that the seeds inside are spread over the country. Flowers are brightly coloured to attract bees. Plants need bees to carry pollen from one flower to another. The green colour of leaves is also vital for plant life.

Plant colours are nearly always pigments (see page 5). This means that the colours can be taken out and used for dyes. Many pigments fade in bright light. However, iridescent animal colours (see page 24), cannot be removed. Because iridescent colours are produced by layers and not chemicals, they do not fade.

A bumble bee homes in on a bright pink rose. The sacs on its legs are bulging with pollen collected from other flowers.

Green for energy?

Plants use their leaves to collect light energy from the Sun and to make food for themselves. The green in their leaves is a pigment called **chlorophyll**. Chlorophyll traps energy from sunlight and uses it to change **carbon dioxide** gas in the air into plant food, such as sugar. Not just any colour light will do. It must be red, orange and blue light. Green light is not useful for plants, so they reflect it. That is why plants look green.

These nasturtium plants have bright orange flowers to attract bees and large green leaves to change the Sun's energy into food.

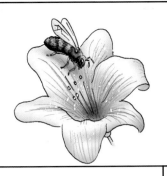

A song thrush enjoys a meal of red berries from a currant bush.

Light experiment

ONION DYE

1 Put the onion peel into the water and bring it to the boil.

2 Using a large fork, carefully dip the cloth in the boiling water for about one minute. The onion peel will dye the cloth yellow.

You need
- A piece of white cloth, 15cm × 15cm
- The brown peel from a medium-sized onion
- A saucepan of water

Good relations

Some plants and animals need each other for their survival. Many plants have brightly coloured flowers to attract insects. The flowers produce sweet nectar for the insects to eat. But each flower has only a little nectar, so an insect has to visit many plants to get a good meal! As it moves from flower to flower, the insect gets dusted with pollen, spreading it from one flower to another. This is what plants need to form their seeds.

Leaves are not always bright green. The bougainvillaea plant grows pink leaves round its flowers to attract bees.

27

Changing colour

Many parts of plants change colour slowly. Fruit and berries are often green when they are unripe and then turn yellow, red or black as they ripen. Red and black fruit contain strong pigments from which dyes can be made. Leaves change colour slowly in the autumn. The green chlorophyll (see page 26) in them is broken down and used up by the plant before its leaves die.

Animals can change colour more quickly. Often an animal changes its colour to match its surroundings so that it is camouflaged. Chameleons, flat fish and squid are good at this and can change colour in a few minutes or even seconds.

In the spring, beech leaves are full of green chlorophyll which gathers red, orange and blue light from the Sun. Green light is reflected.

Spot the difference!

A desert chameleon lies motionless on the rocks, hoping its camouflage will make it invisible to enemies. The grey and black markings make its shape difficult to see.

When you get close, the chameleon realizes that the game is up! Suddenly it turns black all over, opens its yellow mouth, coils its tail and puffs up its body to look as big and fierce as it can.

Beech leaves lose all their chlorophyll in autumn and are no longer any use to the tree, so they fall off.

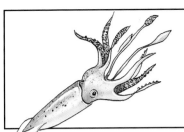

How is it done?

Animals change colour by using cells in their bodies called **chromatophores**. Chromatophores are full of dark pigment. The animal can make the cells expand as black blobs to cover its original body colour. By expanding its chromatophores in patches, an animal such as a fish or chameleon can change its colour pattern and disguise its body shape.

You can see the colour-changing cells on this male stickleback's body. They are filled with a dark pigment.

Light seekers

Light is life to plants. Without it plants would soon wither and die. Plants need light because they use its energy to change carbon dioxide gas in the air into food (see pages 26-27). In dark places plants grow towards the light. They are able to do this even though they have no eyes to see the light. Plant cells which are in the shade or darkness grow more quickly than those cells which are in the light. This uneven growth of the plant's cells pushes the stem over, making it bend towards the light. Some plants actually turn their stems in order to follow the Sun as it moves across the sky during the day.

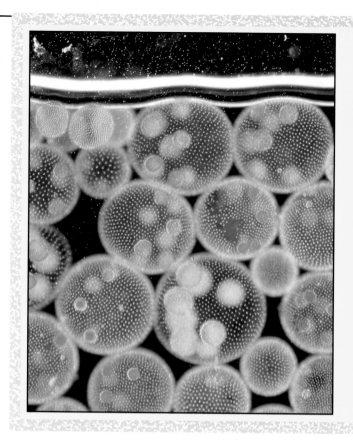

Racing for the light

Plants can grow in darkness for only a short time, using food stored in their roots. The yellow shoots of ground ivy in this picture grew in darkness behind the bark of the log. They grew long and thin as they raced to reach the light.

Light or dark?

Some tiny animals need light just as plants do. These tiny creatures are green coloured and live in water. When the Sun shines they rise to the surface to use the Sun's light energy. Other sorts of animals hide from the light. Woodlice are normally only active at night. If you disturb them they run away towards dark places.

Volvox are creatures like tiny green balls that live in ponds. When the Sun shines, they swim to the surface to collect energy from its light.

Light experiment

SPUD SPECTACULAR!

You need
- A sprouting potato
- A cardboard box

1 Place the potato at one end of the box. Make a 2cm hole in the top of the box at the opposite end.

2 As the shoots grow, they will seek the light and may even grow through the hole in the box.

Reach for the sky

Plants also move their leaves towards light. If you lie on your back under a beech tree in the summer, you will find that you can see only a few chinks of sky. This is because the leaves have moved to catch as much sunlight as possible.

Potatoes send out shoots like fingers which reach for the light above the ground.

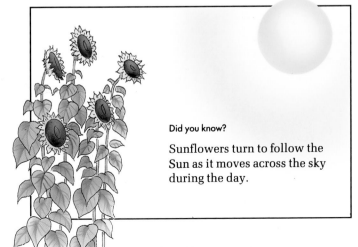

Did you know?

Sunflowers turn to follow the Sun as it moves across the sky during the day.

Light words

Camouflage The colours of animals that make them difficult to see in their surroundings.

Carbon dioxide A gas made of oxygen and carbon.

Chlorophyll The green substance in plants that absorbs energy from the Sun.

Chromatophore A special kind of cell, containing pigment, in some animals' skins.

Converge To meet or come together at one point.

Diverge To spread out from one point.

Electro-magnetic A kind of energy that travels through space as heat, light, X-rays or radio waves.

Focal length The distance between a lens and the image it makes of a distant object.

Galaxies Huge groups of stars.

Interfere To disturb or get in the way of something.

Iridescent Having a surface that shines or glitters with different colours.

Iris The coloured part of the eye.

Lens A piece of transparent material with curved surfaces which can focus light to make an image.

Luminous Shining or glowing.

Pigment Chemical substances that cause animals, plants, rocks or paints to be coloured.

Pupil The hole in the iris of the eye that lets light in.

Radiate To spread out in all directions from a central point.

Refraction The bending of light which happens when rays pass from one transparent substance (such as air) to another (such as water).

Scattered Spread out in all directions.

Index

PICTURE CREDITS

All photographs are by Kim Taylor and Jane Burton except for those supplied by Zefa 10-11 (Moon), 12 (Saturn), 22-23 (rainbow).